Experiencing
God's Presence

Other Women of Faith Bible Studies

WOMEN OF FAITH SM
BIBLE STUDY SERIES

Experiencing
God's Presence

Written by
JANET KOBOBEL GRANT

General Editor
TRACI MULLINS

ZondervanPublishingHouse
Grand Rapids, Michigan

A Division of HarperCollins*Publishers*

Experiencing God's Presence
Copyright © 1998 by Women of Faith, Inc.

Requests for information should be addressed to:

ZondervanPublishingHouse
Grand Rapids, Michigan 49530

ISBN: 0-310-21343-6

General Editor, Traci Mullins
Cover and interior illustration by Jim Dryden
Interior design by Sue Vandenberg Koppenol

Printed in the United States of America

98 99 00 01 02 03 04 /❖ EP/ 10 9 8 7 6 5 4 3 2 1

CONTENTS

FOREWORD

The best advice I ever received was in 1955. I was twenty-three. Somebody had the good sense to say to me, "Luci, if you want to give yourself a gift, learn all you can about the Bible. Start going to a Bible class and don't stop until you have some knowledge under your belt. You won't be sorry." Having just graduated from college, I was living with my parents, and together we drove more than twenty miles to attend that class. We went four nights a week for two years. I've *never* been sorry.

Nothing I've ever done or learned has meant more to me than those classes. Unless I was on my deathbed, I didn't miss. I went faithfully, took notes, absorbed everything like a sponge, asked questions relentlessly, and loved *every* minute! (I probably drove the teacher crazy.)

Today, more than forty years later, this wonderful storehouse of truth is my standard for living, giving, loving, and learning. It is my Rock and Fortress, the pattern for enjoying abundant life on earth, and for all eternity. I know what I believe, and why. I'm open to change on my tastes, personal opinions, even some of my choices. But change my biblical convictions? No way! They're solid and secure, based on God's inerrant, enduring, and unchanging Word. There's nothing like learning God's truth. As he says, it sets you free.

Women of Faith Bible studies are designed to help you deal with everyday problems and issues concerning you. Experienced and wise women who, like the rest of us, want to know God intimately, have written these lessons. They encourage us to dig into the Scriptures, read them carefully, and respond to thought-provoking questions. We're invited to memorize certain verses as sources of support and guidance, to hide his Word in our heads and hearts.

The clever ideas in these studies make me smile. The stories move my spirit. There are valuable suggestions in dealing with others, quotations that cause me to stop and think. The purpose of every activity is to put "some knowledge under your belt" about the Bible and its relevance for life *this very day.*

Give yourself a gift. Grab your Bible, a pencil, notepad, cup of coffee . . . maybe even a friend . . . and get started. I assure you—you'll *never* be sorry.

LUCI SWINDOLL

HOW TO USE THIS GUIDE

Women of Faith Bible studies are designed to take you on a journey toward a more intimate relationship with Christ by bringing you together with your sisters in the faith. We all want to continue to grow in our Christian lives, to please God, to be a vital part of our families, churches, and communities. But too many of us have tried to grow alone. We haven't found enough places where we feel safe to share our heartaches and joys and hopes. We haven't known how to support and be supported by other women in ways that really make a difference. Perhaps we haven't had the tools.

The guide you are about to use will give you the tools you need to explore a fundamental aspect of your walk with God *with* other women who want to grow, too. You'll not only delve into Scripture and consider its relevance to your everyday life, but you'll also get to know other women's questions, struggles, and victories—many similar, some quite different from your own. This guide will give you permission to be yourself, to share honestly, to care for one another's wounds, and laugh together when you take yourselves too seriously.

Each of the six lessons in this guide is divided into six sections. Most you'll discuss as a group; others you'll cover on your own during the week between meetings.

A Moment for Quiet Reflection. The questions in this section are meant to be answered in a few minutes of privacy sometime before you join your group each week. You may already carve out a regular time of personal reflection in your days, so you've experienced the refreshment and insight these times bring to your soul. However, if words like "quiet," "reflection," and "refreshment" have become unfamiliar to you, let this guide get you started with the invaluable practice of setting aside personal time to think, to rest, to pray. Sometimes the answers you write down to the questions in this section will be discussed as a group when you come together; other times they'll just give you something to ponder deep within. Don't neglect this important reflection time each week, and include enough time to read the introduction to the lesson so you'll be familiar with its focus.

Knowing God's Heart. The questions in this section will take you into the Bible, where you and the women in your group can discover God's heart and mind on the subject at hand. You'll do the Bible study together, reading the Scriptures aloud and sharing your understanding of the passage so all of you can learn together what God has to say about your own heart and life, right now. While you don't need to complete the study questions prior to each group session, it will be helpful for you to read through this part of the lesson beforehand so you can begin thinking about your answers. There is a lot to cover in each lesson, so being somewhat familiar with the content before your meetings will save your group time when you actually do your study together.

Friendship Boosters. A big part of why you've come together is to deepen your friendships with other women and to support each other in meaningful ways. The questions and activities in this section are designed to link you together in bonds of friendship, faith, and joy. Whether you are meeting the other women in your group for the first time or are old friends, this section will boost the quality and pleasure in your relationships as well as give you opportunities to support each other in practical ways.

Just for Fun. God's plan for our lives certainly isn't all work and no play! Central to being a woman of faith is cultivating a joyful spirit, a balanced perspective, and an ability to enjoy life because of God's faithfulness and sovereignty. Every week you'll be given an idea or activity that will encourage you to enjoy your journey, laugh, and lighten your load as you travel the path toward wholehearted devotion together.

Praying Together. Nothing is more important than asking God to help you and your friends as you learn how to live out his truths in your lives. Each time you get together you'll want to spend some time talking to him about your individual and mutual concerns.

Making It Real in Your Own Life. You'll respond to these questions or activities on your own after group meetings, but don't consider them just an afterthought. This section is critical because it will help you discover more ways to apply what you've learned and discussed to your own life in the days and weeks ahead. This section will be a key to making God's liberating truths more real to you personally.

In each section, space is provided after each question for you to record your answers, as well as thoughts stimulated by others' answers during group discussion. While you can gain wisdom from completing parts of this guide on your own, you'll miss out on a lot of the power—and the fun!—of making it a group experience.

One woman should be designated as the group facilitator, but she needn't have any training in leading a Bible study or discussion group. The facilitator will just make sure the discussion stays on track, and there are specific notes to help her in the "Leader's Guide" section at the back of this book. Keeping your group size to between four and eight participants is ideal because then it will be possible for everyone to share each week. The length of time you'll need to complete the lessons together will depend largely on how much the participants talk, so the group facilitator will need to monitor the time to keep it under ninety minutes. The facilitator can also speed up or slow down the group time by choosing to skip some discussion questions or concentrate longer on others. If you decide to do this study in

INTRODUCTION
Face-to-Face

Relationships are fascinating labyrinths. That's why, during an unresolved argument, a wife can write her husband a note that reads, "I hate you. Love, Margo." Or why we love to be with our children yet feel relief when they snuggle into bed at last. Or why we yearn to visit our parents and then become childlike and pouty as soon as we sit down for our first meal with them. Or why we buy a handsome Christmas present for our friend with all the generosity in our heart but feel disappointed if her gift didn't seem to require the same amount of careful thought.

The people in our lives cause us to rejoice and lament. We fret over them and then fret with them when a problem stares us down. We at times harbor resentments and then later seek safe harbor with the very people we've resented.

If our human bonds cause such a knot of responses, imagine how much more complex our relationship with God is. We are like him yet so unlike him. He is knowable yet mysterious. Some days he seems so present and others so absent. Sometimes we don't seem to be able to move past the most basic of questions about him: *Who is he? What is he like? What does he think of me?* Yet we are eager to know this and much more. *How can I celebrate his presence in my life when my circumstances are bitter? How can I please him when the path ahead is foggy and he isn't communicating clearly? Can I feel loved again if I fall and muddy myself up miserably?*

When we look to the Bible for answers to these questions, we are often drawn to the man Job. Job had his own struggles with figuring out how to experience God. After Job flung every question he could imagine

13

heavenward, God actually gave Job the audience he had been longing for. But God didn't engage Job in the Q & A he had anticipated. Instead, God reversed the roles and asked all the questions rather than answering any. And his questions were hard: *Where were you when I laid the earth's foundations? Who set the sea's boundaries? Have you ever given the morning orders?* Well, the quiz lasted a long time (several chapters in the book of Job). Job failed. As a matter of fact, he was stunned into silence. (Ever felt that way with God?) But rather than being dismayed or disheartened, Job rejoiced. For the questions themselves had been instructive. And Job came away from it all with a firmer grasp on how to experience God.

Not that he had found the Seven Steps to a Richer Relationship. It's never that easy. The word *experience* is defined in the Oxford English Dictionary as "to put to the test; to learn (a fact) by experience; to find." Job— and we—experience God when the facts we have accumulated about him and how he relates to us are put to the test. Then, ah yes, then we experience those facts in ways we never have before. That's what knowing God is all about. In fact, Job says at the end of God's quiz, "My ears had heard of you but now my eyes have seen you."

Isn't that just like God? We think we need answers to our questions, but he realizes we need to be quizzed. We think we can know God through paved avenues; he sneaks up on us on narrow paths we didn't even know existed. We want Rules for Relating; he declares he just wants a relationship. Thus we come face-to-face with God. All he asks is that we enter into his presence with open hearts, cradling in our hands our minuscule seed of faith.

That's the lesson learned by the people whose shoulders we'll peer over in the upcoming lessons. These biblical characters found themselves nestled under God's wing when they praised him, even when their praises were tinged with sadness; set time apart to be with him; gave to others for Jesus' sake, even when there was little to share; wrestled through the puzzles of life with him; humbly admitted their shortcomings, even when others offered them compliments; and rejoiced in God's amazing grace, even when others couldn't believe God could forgive such abhorrent sins.

So set your heart to encounter God whether you have bounteous praise to offer him or a soul bereft of riches. He'll satisfy you and enrich your spirit as he reveals himself to you. Guaranteed.

Celebrate Him!

M ost of us use any excuse for a party. One woman threw a Spring Is Coming Picnic to deal with midwinter doldrums. Her green living room carpet served as the lawn, and she even purchased plastic ants to toss onto the tablecloth spread with springtime treats. Another woman gave her dog a birthday party and invited friends over to play Pin the Tail on the Puppy (a paper puppy, not the real item) and other canine-related games. Why, the whole concept of Thank God It's Friday sounds like a party waiting to happen once a week!

Yes, we're always on the lookout for reasons to celebrate. God seems to approve, for the Bible reports a number of festivities: David's celebration when the ark is moved into the city (dancing, music, and food abounded); the wedding feast with the finest wine money couldn't buy; the regular family fetes Job's children had; the end-of-sheep-shearing party Nabal refused to invite David to; the Passover feast to celebrate God's mercy.

Despite our propensity to party and God's institution of some celebrations of his own, we seem to spend little time experiencing God through celebration. How do we establish a personal tradition of praising him? We'll take a look at a couple of ways people in the Bible did just that. One is a Grand Opening that included weeping and rejoicing; the other shows us how to throw a grand opening in our own hearts.

> *On this mountain the LORD Almighty will prepare a feast of rich food for all peoples, a banquet of aged wine— the best of meats and the finest of wines.*
>
> ISAIAH 25:6

A Moment for Quiet Reflection

1. Find a quiet corner in which you can relax, maybe sip a cup of tea, and jot down thoughts as they occur to you. View this time and place as the setting to meet with and experience God.

2. List the different types of celebrations you can recall ever attending.

3. What were your favorites? Why?

4. How could you incorporate your favorite aspects of a celebration into your relationship with God? (Remember, you don't have to celebrate your spiritual relationship by yourself. That's what the term "corporate worship" means.)

5. Make a plan to include some of those ideas into your times with God in the weeks ahead.

Knowing God's Heart

1. Share a celebration idea from your reflection time with the group. This is one way you can begin to get to know each other, and you might just pick up some ideas that hadn't occurred to you.

2. Praising God is a key element in celebrating your relationship with him. Psalm 147 provides us with a list of reasons to praise him. Read over the entire psalm, and find ten reasons it gives to praise God.

3. Discuss five ways to praise God suggested in this psalm.

4. What are some of the specific ways you have praised God and how have they led you to experience him more deeply?

5. Brainstorm ideas for creatively using the five ways to praise God described in the psalm during your personal times with God.

6. In Ezra 3, a corporate time of celebrating God takes place when the Israelites have a ground-breaking ceremony to mark the laying of the temple's foundation. The temple had been destroyed decades before when Israel was overrun by the Babylonians, and the Israelites were carted off as prisoners. Those who attended the ceremony were returning exiles or the children of exiles. According to verses 10–11, what elements were used to make the celebration special?

7. Verses 12–13 report the crowd expressed a mixture of joy and tears. What occasions today can you think of in which people feel such a range of emotions?

8. What does this passage's scene tell us about "appropriate" emotions when we praise God?

9. List as many reasons as you can think of that these people had to praise God.

10. What does the psalm and the passage from Ezra teach you about the meaning of "praising God"?

11. How can you enrich your relationship with God through praising him?

> *Have you noticed that we are laughter and tears, dirges and dances, jubilations and consternations, hallelujahs and woes?*
>
> Patsy Clairmont

Friendship Boosters

Declare the upcoming week Celebrate Friendship Week. Exchange phone numbers and addresses. Keep your eyes open for little tokens of friendship (a bookmark or a card), quotes about friendship, or cartoons or jokes about friends. Each day call a different person in the group and tell her what you've discovered. Start out by calling the person who sat on your right and work your way around the circle. Or send that person the item. Use this week to concentrate on growing closer to one another.

Just for Fun

Plan a time to attend a local celebration together. It could be a store's grand opening (ooh, sales!), an ethnic group's festival, a circus, a chili cook-off, or whatever is happening in your community. Use your imagination and dare to do something you haven't done before. Pay attention to the various emotions within and around you and what they tell you about the nature of celebration.

When I was a child, my Sunday-school teacher always told me, "God's blessing bucket is bottomless."
BARBARA JOHNSON

Praying Together

Name some songs of praise you especially like. As a group, pick two of them and sing them as your prayer together. If you have trouble choosing, you might want to sing a couple of familiar Christmas songs such as "Joy to the World" or "O Come All Ye Faithful."

> *Adoration is the lifting up of the heart and mind to God, asking nothing but to enjoy God's presence.*
> THE BOOK OF COMMON PRAYER

Making It Real in Your Own Life

1. Nature is a luxurious place to look for reasons to celebrate God. It's loaded with lovely sights—and sometimes silly ones, too. (Ever watch a squirrel and a dog having a "discussion" over whom the backyard belongs to?) Keep a list this week of what you see in nature that causes you to celebrate.

2. At the end of the week, look over your list and write a psalm, praising God for how wonderfully he has expressed himself in nature and how this enriches your personal experience of him. To get in the right frame of mind, you might want to read Psalm 19 and Psalm 95. Relax and think of this as a way to let God know you recognize how awesome he is.

Solitary Refinement

Reflections surround us. We check our reflection in the mirror in the morning (and then realize what a big mistake THAT was!). We admire the mountains and trees reflected so perfectly in a smooth lake. Children reflect their parents (that's good news and bad news!). We polish the silver (our one piece inherited from Aunt Gladys) and admire our reflection in the finished work. We catch our reflection in a shop window as we walk by and are almost surprised to see ourselves looking back. We reflect our taste in the clothes we wear, the way we decorate our homes, and the cars we drive.

But of all the reflections in our lives, the most important is the way we reflect who God is to others. Our actions speak volumes to people about Jesus. That's a responsibility and a privilege, isn't it? If we're to reflect the Lord as accurately as possible, we need to spend time with him, reflecting (thinking about) who he is to us. Knowing him better, in turn, results in experiencing him more profoundly. And that's what solitary time with him does for us.

Once we settle down, quiet the noise within and the noise without, and spend time tuning in to God, we come away from that golden communication refined. We've given up our burdens, shored up our faith, lifted up our prayers, stored up Scripture in our hearts, and now we're shined up to reflect God. Our internal experience with God leads to an external expression of him.

Today, our focus is on a man who felt the burden of reflecting God. Moses climbed up a mountain to discuss his concerns with the Lord and came down with much more than he could have imagined.

> *Women need solitude in order to find again*
> *the true essence of themselves: that firm strand*
> *which will be the indispensable center of a*
> *whole web of human relationships.*
> ANNE MORROW LINDBERGH

A Moment for Quiet Reflection

1. Write the word "solitude" down the side of a page, one letter per line. Create a poem beginning each line with the appropriate letter that reflects the benefits of spending time alone with God. For example,

> *Silence fills my soul with light*
> *Only You could shut out my night . . .*

Or, if you would rather, just jot thoughts after each letter; they don't have to fit together into a poem.

2. List all the reasons you can think of that keep you from experiencing the benefits of time alone with God. Some of these could be external, such as circumstances that get in the way. Others might be internal, such as emotions or the inability to stay still for any length of time.

3. Turn your acrostic poem or thoughts into a prayer in which you discuss with God why you want to experience these things but why it is hard for you to do so. When you've finished, sit in silence for at least three minutes and listen to any response from God. Write down what you hear.

Knowing God's Heart

1. Shortly after the bored Israelites built the golden calf out of their melted jewelry, Moses and the Lord had a private discussion about God's Chosen. It wasn't pretty. God told Moses what he thought about them in Exodus 33:5. Moses, in turn, had his own misgivings, which are recorded in Exodus 33:12–13. What concerned God? What concerned Moses?

2. God mentions in verses 12 and 17 that he knows Moses by name. Why do you think he does that?

3. Do you think Moses makes his request in verse 18 despite God's words of comfort or because of them? Why?

4. In verse 19, what are three ways God uses to show Moses his glory?

5. Why do you think God chose those ways?

6. In verses 21 and 22, in what ways does God show his love and respect for Moses?

7. What do these verses suggest about the potential benefits of spending time alone with God?

8. God then gives Moses a second set of the Ten Commandments (Exodus 34), Moses having smashed the first in his anger over the golden calf. According to verse 27, what did Moses gain from spending time with God that you could expect to gain as well?

9. Verse 29 tells us about another effect of spending time with God. How do you think this could be applied to our lives?

10. Read 2 Corinthians 3:18. What other expressions of God are available to us that Moses didn't have?

11. What about Moses' story speaks most clearly to you about experiencing God in solitary time?

Friendship Boosters

Set aside some time in the near future to be with God in a concentrated, focused way. It could be as small as half an hour listening to a praise tape while you soak in the tub or as large as a weekend retreat, just you and God. Team up with another woman in the group and share your plans with each other. Brainstorm what would be meaningful content for this specially designated time. Afterward, get together and reflect on what you learned about experiencing God during your solitary time.

> *It is not needful always to be in church to be with God. We make a chapel of our heart, to which we can from time to time withdraw to have gentle, humble, loving communion with Him.*
>
> BROTHER LAWRENCE

Just for Fun

Photographs reflect how we see the world. Spend at least an hour this week with the person in the group whose first name comes after yours in the alphabet. Bring a camera and take photos of things or people you think reflect God in the world. Think about not only the beautiful (such as a flower or sunset) but also the fun (a child standing on her head) and the ridiculously creative (a "Beware of the Dog" sign with a sleepy-eyed beagle standing next to it). Get your photos developed and choose the ones you like best to share with the group next week. (Don't worry about whether your photography is good; the point is to look at the world from a different perspective and to share that with each other.)

Praying Together

Write on a slip of paper one thing you want to change about the way you spend time with God (besides wanting to spend more time). Give it to the person sitting on your left. Go around the group, each of you praying aloud for the woman's request you've been handed.

> When our hearts are tenderly responsive . . . and it suits his greater plan, then the Lord will lift the thin veil that separates us. And we will be stunned to realize that he has been closer than our own breath all along.
>
> PATSY CLAIRMONT

Making It Real in Your Own Life

1. Look back at the response you heard from God during your "Moment for Quiet Reflection." What changes can you make based on that response that would enable you to more freely have solitary time with God?

2. How can you specifically institute those changes?

3. Commit to spending a certain amount of time with God each day this week. Structure the time to include (1) praying, during which you both speak and listen; (2) reading Scripture and asking yourself, *What does this passage teach me about God?* (3) asking God how you can reflect him in a specific situation that day (or the next day, if your time is during the evening); (4) sitting in silence after asking God to reveal himself to you. Try to increase the time spent in silence each day.

> *Every morning, lean thine arms awhile*
> *Upon the window sill of heaven,*
> *And gaze upon the Lord.*
> *Then, with that vision in thy heart,*
> *Turn strong to meet the day.*
>
> ANONYMOUS

Giving Your All

When you think of a generous person, who comes to mind? Perhaps your friend who slept in the chair by your hospital bed, the better to keep watch over you. Or maybe your sister, who fills your refrigerator with orange juice, milk, and veggies to welcome you home each time you return from a business trip. Then again, maybe it's the person who has prayed for you over the years with a persistence and care that is touching.

We all know that giving of ourselves brings bounteous blessings to others and increases our joy as well. But sometimes we cry out that we have no more to give, that we have exceeded the limits allowed. Sometimes we need to call a moratorium, to listen carefully when our interior being makes these proclamations, for ignoring them can have large and long-lasting consequences.

What happens, though, when God makes it clear we are to give beyond what we think we are able? Then giving becomes an act of faith—and another way to experience God. As we look to him for the provision to give to others, we discover a special closeness to God. And we understand more what it cost him to be generous toward us.

That's the situation the individuals in our lesson today faced. Their responses teach us how generosity, faith, and obedience often come packaged like a picnic tucked in a basket of blessing.

> *A generous man will prosper; he who refreshes*
> *others will himself be refreshed.*
>
> PROVERBS 11:25

A Moment
for Quiet Reflection

1. Write down the best gift you ever received (from someone besides God) and why you would rate it that way. If you have trouble choosing just one, list two or three.

2. What's the best gift you ever gave? List two or three, if one doesn't stand out to you. Why do you rate it (or them) that way?

3. What is the costliest gift you ever gave? What did it cost you—time, money, personal comfort?

4. List five qualities of a gift that make it special.

5. What are the five best gifts God has given you? Thank him for them.

Knowing God's Heart

1. Tell the group about one of the best gifts you ever received and why you think of it that way.

2. How many of the gifts mentioned were special because some sacrifice was involved in giving them?

3. Read Mark 6:30–44. List the emotions you might have felt if you were one of the disciples in this situation.

4. Now list the emotions you might have felt if you were the one to give up your lunch of fish and bread.

5. What lessons do you think Jesus wanted the disciples (and us) to learn about experiencing God?

6. Retell the story as it would have unfolded if Jesus had followed his disciples' advice.

7. Read Mark 6:45–52. What does the disciples' inability to learn from the feeding of the five thousand teach us about what we can do differently?

8. Since the disciples didn't "get it" when Jesus fed the five thousand, he gives them Lesson 2, walking on the water. What does Lesson 2 tell us about how he responds when we don't figure out what we're supposed to learn?

9. What blessings do you think the boy who gave his lunch experienced that the disciples missed out on? (See John 6:5–13.)

10. Which of those blessings especially motivates you to respond with generosity when God asks you, in faith and obedience, to do something for others? Why?

> *Sometimes I forget the sweet truth that God's Father-heart delights in giving good gifts to his children.*
>
> MARILYN MEBERG

Friendship Boosters

Write your name at the top of a sheet of paper and pass your sheet to the person on your right. That person will write down one thing she appreciates about you and how you experience God. Continue to pass the sheets until yours comes back to you.

Just for Fun

1. Share your favorite photo(s) from your picture-taking venture last week—and the adventures you experienced while taking the pics.

2. Team up with the person sitting across from you. Together create a tea basket consisting of a couple of tea bags, packets of sugar or honey, and three cups and spoons. Visit someone who doesn't get to interact much with others (an elderly person, a new mother, a shut-in). Call ahead to let the person know you are coming for tea and assure her you don't want her to do one thing to clean up for you; you're coming to give to her. When you arrive, heat up the water and prepare the tea. Treat the person you are visiting as your guest. Chat for awhile—one hour at most—and center the conversation on the person you're visiting. If it's an older person, ask questions about her childhood or ways she has seen God's generosity in her life. Make this a time to give to someone else. If it's appropriate, end your time with the person in prayer. Afterward, talk about ways giving to that person enabled you to experience God.

Praying Together

Spend your time in prayer together bringing others outside the group before the throne of grace. As you go around the room, give a prayer request for someone besides yourself.

> *Love: a basket of bread*
> *from which to eat*
> *for years to come;*
> *good loaves, fragrant and warm,*
> *miraculously multiplied:*
> *the basket never empty*
> *the bread never stale.*
>
> CATHERINE DE VINCK

Making It Real
in Your Own Life

1. For your Scripture reading this week, use your concordance to look up verses on giving. As you look up the verses, read them in their context. Make a list of ways God gives to us and ways God wants us to give to others.

2. Ask the Lord how he wants you to put feet to the discoveries you make as you study. Write down at least one specific action you will take.

> An African boy gave his missionary teacher an exquisite seashell as a Christmas gift. The lad had walked miles for it, to a special bay, the only place where such shells were found. "How wonderful of you to have traveled so far for this present," said the teacher. The boy's eyes shone as he replied, "Long walk part of gift."
>
> READER'S DIGEST

Grappling with God

Doesn't wrestling seem like a guy thing? You know, Big Time Wrestling with burly men hurling each other through the air and landing with aplomb, little boys wriggling around on the living room rug.

Well, we women wrestle, too. We wrestle with the grocery bags as we lug them in the house, with the kids as we dunk them into the bathtub, and with God. We wrestle with God over how to resolve a sticky relationship, how to love someone who is acting unlovable, and sometimes we even grapple with God to get him to do what we think he ought.

Fortunately we serve a gracious God who allows us to wrestle with him—even to foolishly try to manipulate him to move in a particular direction. When we get down on the mat with God, he graciously reveals truth to us—and gives us an experience of him we'll never forget.

The biblical character Jacob provides us with some insights when he wrestles, quite literally, with the Almighty.

> *Do not let it be imagined that one must remain silent about one's feelings of rebellion in order to enter into dialogue with God. Quite the opposite is the truth: it is precisely when one expresses them that a dialogue of truth begins.*
>
> PAUL TOURNIER

A Moment
for Quiet Reflection

1. Create a reprise of various struggles you have had with God. Think back to when God began to call you to be his child; did you struggle? How?

2. What faith struggles did you encounter as a new believer?

3. Over the months or years since entering into a relationship with Christ, what things have you tried to convince God to "give" you?

4. What techniques have you used to try to get God to do what you wanted him to?

5. Are you grappling with God over something today? If so, what?

6. Tell God how you feel about your relationship with him after examining it under the light of struggles past and present.

Knowing God's Heart

1. Jacob was a determined man. When he set out to get something, he got it. He wrested his father's blessing from the
   blinded man, the blessing that belonged to Jacob's elder
   brother, Esau. He got the bride he wanted, although he had
   to work for his father-in-law for fourteen years and was
   tricked into marrying Rachel's sister, Leah, first. Then,
   through trickery, he got the largest portion of the flock he
   shared with his father-in-law. Yes, when Jacob set out to
   get something, he got it. We pick up his story as he travels
   back to the land he was to receive because of his father's
   blessing. He is moving a great entourage of flocks, belong-
   ings, slaves, wives, and children. Read Genesis 32:3–5.
   What is Jacob's approach with his brother—who had
   threatened to kill Jacob decades before when Jacob
   cheated him—to persuade Esau to accept him peacefully?

2. In verses 6–12, what does Jacob say to convince God to
   keep him safe from his brother's possible wrath and
   revenge?

3. In verses 13–21, how does Jacob attempt to make the offer of peaceful coexistence more enticing to Esau?

4. Read verses 22–32. In what ways was Jacob consistent with previous methods of dealing with others?

5. Did his approach work? Why or why not?

6. Why do you think God caused a wound that would make Jacob limp for the rest of his life?

7. How do you think Jacob felt about that wound?

8. Has God ever "wounded" you during a wrestling match? If so, describe the wound and what you learned from the match.

9. Read Genesis 33:1–9. In what ways does Esau differ from Jacob?

10. This segment of Jacob's life is concluded in Genesis 33:18–20. The name of the altar means "mighty is the God of Israel." Why do you think Jacob chose that name?

11. What does Jacob's saga tell us about God's response to our grappling with him?

12. If you are currently wrestling with God over something, what does this story suggest about how he's viewing you in the struggle?

> *O God of Jacob, who knew how*
> *to change supplanters then, so now*
> *deal, I pray, with this my son,*
> *though he may limp*
> *when Thou art done.*
>
> RUTH BELL GRAHAM
> OF HER PRODIGAL SON

Friendship Boosters

In Genesis 25:26, we learn that the name "Jacob" means "he grasps the heel" (a born wrestler!) or figuratively, "he deceives." The name "Israel" means "he struggles with God," which is the name God gives Jacob during their wrestling match. It seems to indicate a transformation in Jacob's character and approach to life as a result of his encounter with God.

In the spirit of understanding our names and the possibilities of being transformed by our names, look up each woman's name in a baby book that provides names' meanings. (Your local library will probably have such a book if no one in the group does.) Explain why your name was given to you or why you chose the names you did for your children.

Just for Fun

If Jacob was good at one thing, it was coloring outside the lines of life. Pair off with the person whose last four digits of her Social Security number are closest to yours and plan a time to go buy some crayons and a coloring book together (you might each want your own!), and spend some time coloring together this week. While you're coloring, talk about what you're learning regarding wrestling with God and experiencing him. If coloring isn't your thing, pursue some other childhood activity such as playing jacks or swinging.

Praying Together

Pray aloud as a group the following traditional prayer. It's a prayer that can help us to have a balanced view of ourselves—certainly something Jacob struggled with.

Lord God Almighty, I ask not to be enrolled amongst the earthly great and rich, but to be numbered with the spiritually blessed.

Make it my present, supreme, persevering concern to obtain those blessings which are spiritual in their nature, eternal in their continuance, satisfying in their possession.

Preserve me from a false estimate of the whole or a part of my character; may I pay regard to my principles as well as my conduct, my motives as well as my actions.

Help me never to mistake the excitement of my passions for the renewing of the Holy Spirit, never to judge my religion by occasional impressions and impulses, but by my constant and prevailing disposition.

May my heart be right with thee, and my life as becometh the gospel.

May I maintain a supreme regard to another and better world, and feel and confess myself a stranger and a pilgrim here.

Afford me all the direction, defense, support, and consolation my journey hence requires, and grant me a mind stayed on thee.

Give me a large abundance of the supply of the Spirit of Jesus, that I may be prepared for every duty, love thee in all my mercies, submit to thee in every trial, trust thee when walking in darkness, have peace in thee amidst life's changes.

Lord, I believe. Help thou my unbelief and uncertainties.

Lord, make me content with who I am, what I have, and where I find myself. Because it is here, at this point, that you will meet me and, if necessary, change me.

LUCI SWINDOLL

Making It Real
in Your Own Life

1. Prepare an "offering" for a Jacob in your life. Often we resist people whom we know are trying to manipulate us in some way. Show the kindness and forgiveness that Esau displayed by giving your "Jacob" something that would please him or her. This may take prayerful preparation on your part to carry out with a sincere heart. It will do your heart good.

2. Many of the psalms are reflections of the writers' struggles with God. Find a psalm that especially reflects your grappling with God and read it every day this week as a prayer. (Some suggested psalms: 17, 22, 36, 42, or 55.) Note how many of these psalms begin with questions and end with praise. Watch to see how this practice transforms you as you wrestle with him in your praying.

> *God is the enemy whom Jacob fought there by the river, of course, and whom in one way or another we all of us fight—God, the beloved enemy. Our enemy because, before giving us everything, he demands of us everything.*
>
> FREDERICK BUECHNER

Hidden Places of the Heart

*B*aked Alaska fascinates us mostly because hidden underneath that luscious meringue dome lies ice cream that has come out of the oven unscathed. Spiritually, we can sometimes be like that. God takes us through a fiery furnace designed to refine us and shape us more into his image. And while our "meringue" exterior looks as though we've been transformed, in actuality, our heart is cold, untouched by God's hand.

None of us wants to fit that description, but probably at some point in our lives each of us will. We start out with a humble heart, but along the way a core weakness is exposed. We may be as surprised to discover that hidden place in our heart as everyone else is.

Is there anything we can do to avoid such a moment? Can we prepare our hearts to respond to God in ways that lead to a deeper, richer relationship rather than give him an icy reception when we get a little testy? In this lesson, we're going to examine what God has revealed about one man who had a heart condition of that fatal kind—a core of spiritual coldness. As we look at his life, we'll learn how to keep our relationship with God oven-toasty warm and out of the deep freezer.

> *Search me, O God, and know my heart.*
>
> PSALM 139:23

A Moment for Quiet Reflection

1. Write down all the words you can think of in three minutes that include "heart." For example, "lighthearted," "disheartened," and so forth.

2. Put a check mark by the words that describe your heart. If none of them fits, write down words that do.

3. Pray about your heart's condition. Thank God for the times you are lighthearted and happy to be his child. Then ask him to reveal to you any cold or dark spots you need to be aware of that could hinder your ability to experience God.

4. Examine with God your spiritual "fitness" program: Does your soul need more exercise? How have your spiritual eating habits been? Are you getting the spiritual rest you need?

5. Make plans to incorporate into your life—one step at a time—whatever God reveals to you. Begin this week.

Knowing God's Heart

1. Saul was the first king for the Israelites. He was given by God to the people because they insisted they wanted a man to rule them rather than be ruled by God or his prophets. In 1 Samuel 10:17–22 Samuel announces Saul is to be king. Why do you think Saul hid among the baggage? (Keep in mind this wasn't a surprise to him. First Samuel 10:1 describes Saul's anointing by Samuel that took place earlier.)

2. In verses 23–26, Saul is "presented" to the people. What qualities of Saul's heart does verse 27 reveal?

3. Ultimately, Saul ruled for forty-two years. During that time he raised up armies and defeated Israel's enemies. But Saul chose to ignore the regulations for a kingly rule that Samuel had laid out when Saul was publicly proclaimed king. In 1 Samuel 15:1–11, we read of Saul's downfall. What positive qualities does Saul express in this passage?

4. What other qualities does Saul reveal in verses 12–23?

5. Do you think Saul's repentance in verses 24–31 is sincere? Why or why not?

6. Who took Saul's place as king and how was his relationship with God described in Acts 13:22?

7. Based on the passages you've looked at today, list at least six aspects of the heart that can draw us closer to God or pull us away.

8. Which heart-quality do you think is your greatest weakness? (Everyone in the group has to choose one!)

9. How has this quality hindered your experience of God?

10. Discuss what can be done to safeguard yourself from your weaknesses. Be specific about times when you are especially vulnerable and actions you can take. Brainstorm preventive measures as a group.

Friendship Boosters

1. Discuss how you keep your heart responsive in your close relationships (with friends, spouses, children, and others). Share some of the lighthearted things you do as well as some of the more serious. Talk about how those ideas could translate to your relationship with God.

2. Add up the numbers of your house's address (e.g, 3223 would be 3+2+2+3=10) and locate the person in the group whose total matches yours or is the closest. Buy or make something heart-shaped for that person this week to remind her that her goal is to be a woman after God's own heart.

> *Batter my heart, three personed God; . . .*
> *That I may rise and stand, o'erthrow me and bend*
> *Your force to break, blow, burn and make me new.*
> JOHN DONNE

Just for Fun

Select a "queen for the day" from the group by each writing your name on a slip of paper and dropping it into some heart-red object. Have the youngest person in the group draw a name to determine the "queen." Agree on an upcoming day to "celebrate" this person's heart and how she experiences God. Plan something that centers around the heart theme. You might have a high tea with heart-shaped cookies and sandwiches. Or each group member could make a valentine for her expressing some admirable aspect of her heart. Then present them to her over lunch at a restaurant or home that has a room decorated in red. Use your imagination!

Praying Together

Ask one woman to be the prayer leader for the group. She will pray the following prayer, one sentence at a time with pauses of about thirty seconds between each sentence. The pauses will give each of you time to communicate silently with God about that topic. Don't be afraid of the silent spaces but use them to examine your heart and draw closer to God.

Everliving Father, we come before you acknowledging that all we are and all we have is yours.
We come to offer you praise for who you are.
We acknowledge that our love for you is imperfect.
We admit that we have done things that do not honor you.
And we have left undone things you have wanted us to do.
Help us to examine our hearts, to see the flaws and imperfections.
We ask forgiveness for our sins, inadequacies, and presumptions.

Open our eyes, ears, and hearts, that we may grow closer to you through joy and suffering.

Enable us to grow in grace and in our understanding of you.

Keep our hearts open and responsive to the work you wish to do in us.

Enable us to be humble before you.

Now we offer our penitent hearts to you, asking that you be gracious and merciful to us.

In Jesus' name, amen.

> *You show that you are a letter from Christ, the result of our ministry, written not with ink but with the Spirit of the living God, not on tablets of stone but on tablets of human hearts.*
>
> 2 CORINTHIANS 3:3

Making It Real in Your Own Life

1. Read about David's life this week, writing down his heart's strengths and weaknesses as you go along. You could begin in 1 Samuel 16 in which David is anointed king. Or if you would rather read about his later life, you could start in 2 Samuel 1 where David hears of Saul's death. (You probably won't have time to read all about David, since his life is portrayed in considerable detail. Cover as much territory as you have time for.)

2. As you look over your list of David's characteristics, ask yourself what you can learn about the human heart. What does the list tell you about God's response to the heart and how having a right heart leads to experiencing him more?

3. What insights do you gain about your own heart?

4. What would you like to change about your heart? What specific action will you take to do so?

> *Misfortunes one can endure—they come from outside;*
> *they are accidents. But to suffer for one's own faults—*
> *ah, there is the sting of life.*
>
> OSCAR WILDE

Astonishing Grace

*E*ver feel the need for grace? Oh, sure, when you became a Christian you knew you needed amazing grace, but what about since then?

Six-year-old Megan certainly needed it. Her favorite winter pastime was to walk home from school through the park. The cold air seemed to salute her, and the stalwart soldier-trees made her feel like a princess. Rather than walk on the cleared paths, she chose to dance across the park's grass, which was sealed under a crinkly coat of ice.

But one day Megan's reign came to an abrupt end. As she tiptoed home to the sound of "crick" and "crack" from the playful ice, she smashed through a thawed spot and found herself up to her knees in the iciest bathwater it would ever please a princess to encounter.

Pulling her leg from the mushy, iced water, her spirits were dampened considerably. But her biggest problem lay ahead of her: how to explain to her mother what had happened. For Megan's mom had told her repeatedly to walk on the paths, never on the ice. Ignoring her mother's admonition had only added to Megan's secret delight in her walk—until now.

On arriving home, Megan morosely pulled off her waterlogged shoes and socks.

"Megan," her mom said, "how did you get so wet?"

"I don't know," Megan lied, feeling trapped and not at all like a princess who could do whatever she pleased.

"I saw you through the window; I know you were walking on the ice." Then her mom laughed. "I'll bet you'll never do that again! Aren't your toes freezing?"

Astonished, Megan looked up at her mom.

"I'll make you a nice, warm bath. How's that?" Mom said, hugging Megan.

All we like Megan have skipped along, choosing disobedience over responsiveness. And we've often fallen into the ice water as a result. We know we deserve punishment for what we've done. We would like to squirm out of it but can't figure how. Then the person we've offended astonishes us by extending the embrace of forgiveness and grace rather than the hand of anger.

The individual from the Bible we're going to study today did something a lot worse than walk on ice. When he came face-to-face with the person he had offended, he discovered what an astonishing thing grace is. As we all have.

> *Our courteous Lord does not want his servants*
> *to despair even if they fall frequently and grievously.*
> *Our falling does not stop his loving us.*
> JULIAN OF NORWICH

A Moment
for Quiet Reflection

1. Take a few minutes to list situations in which you needed someone to extend grace to you: when you broke something you borrowed, when you failed to keep your word, when you disappointed someone.

2. Now make a list of some times you extended grace to people: when one of your children broke something; when your husband failed to keep his promise; when your mother managed to push all your buttons. Try to recall some lighthearted moments such as Megan and her mom had as well as the serious, hurtful disappointments.

3. How did you feel toward the people who extended grace to you?

4. How did you feel about the people you extended grace to?

5. What insights do these experiences offer about how God feels toward you?

6. What do these experiences make you feel toward God and the grace he offers?

7. As you think about God, you, and others, how would you define grace? Write down your thoughts.

8. Now take a minute to look up the word *grace* in a dictionary or a Bible dictionary. Write down those definitions.

Knowing God's Heart

1. Tell a brief story about a time grace was extended to you or a time you extended it to someone else.

2. Acts 6 and 7 tells the story of Stephen, the first martyr of the church. When called to testify before the Jewish religious council as to whether he blasphemed, Stephen gave a stirring evangelistic message instead. What happened next is recorded in Acts 7:54–8:3. What do we learn about the individual named Saul of Tarsus from this passage?

3. What other qualities are revealed in Acts 9:1–2?

4. In verses 3–9, Jesus reveals himself to Saul. If you were Saul, what would you be thinking about during those three days? List at least five things.

5. Why do you think God made Saul wait three days before restoring his sight?

6. What does that tell you about how God deals with us when we are in need of grace?

7. In verses 10–16, God instructs Ananias to go to Saul. What parts did grace play in this situation for Ananias?

8. How was Ananias most likely to respond to the idea that Saul would take Jesus' name to the Gentiles?

9. Ananias obeys God in verse 17. What do you think it meant to Ananias to call Saul "brother"? How do you think Saul would normally respond to that term?

10. What lessons about extending grace to others do you think Saul learns through his experiences described in verses 18–30?

11. Make a list of five key principles about grace that Saul's story teaches and tell how grace enriches our relationship with God.

12. What amazes you most about grace and why: that it is free? that we don't deserve it? that God expects us to express it to others?

Friendship Boosters

To celebrate the group's time together over the past several weeks, pull out the chalk and head to the driveway. Have each group member draw on the cement things that make her feel lighthearted. Have the rest of the group try to guess what those things are! (If the weather doesn't permit chalk artwork, tape together sheets of paper to create a paper "canvas" for the group to draw on. Spread out your canvas on a table or on the floor and use crayons for your artwork.)

> *Let never day nor night unhallowed pass but*
> *still remember what the Lord hath done.*
> WILLIAM SHAKESPEARE

Just for Fun

Divide into groups of three or four. Have each group come up with as many variations on the use of the word *grace* or a derivation of that word as it can, e.g. "graceful," "gracious," "table grace." The group that loses sponsors a trip to slurp or eat treats— to an ice cream (or yogurt) shop, to the best bakery in town, to Starbucks, wherever! Go right now if you can!

Praying Together

Reading Scripture to God as a prayer can be a very meaningful way to communicate with him. Appoint a leader to read the first line of each verse in Psalm 103. As a group, read the second line aloud. Think about how these verses extol grace and thank God for it as you read, listen, and pray.

> God, lover of souls, swaying considerate scales,
> Complete thy creature dear, O where it fails,
> Being mighty a master, being a father and fond.
> GERARD MANLEY HOPKINS

Making It Real in Your Own Life

1. Read about the effects of grace in the following verses:

- 2 Corinthians 1:12
- Titus 2:11–14
- 1 Peter 4:8–10

2. In what areas of your life do these verses remind you that you need to show grace? To whom do you need to extend grace? Write down each action or change of heart you need to undertake and commit those to the Lord in prayer.

3. Look over the lessons in this study and record below the ways you have encountered God. Put an exclamation mark by the ones that surprised you, a cross by the ones that were reminders of how you and God relate, and an asterisk by the ones you want to explore more on your own. Make plans to do so. You might want to have a personal study (read a book about the topic or do a Bible study using your concordance) or call one of the women from the group and ask her to explore that area with you. Remember, God is full of mysterious, wonderful surprises. He'll richly reward you for spending the time learning more about how to experience him.

But as I raved, and grew more fierce and wild
At every word,
Me thought I heard one calling, "Child";
And I replied, "My Lord."

GEORGE HERBERT

LEADER'S GUIDE

LESSON ONE

Purpose: To learn ways to experience God through praising him.

3. Some of the ways suggested in this psalm to praise God include singing and music; appreciating his handiwork in nature; recognizing his care and provision for us; thanking him; hoping in him as an act of faith.

7. We see people rejoicing and weeping at weddings, funerals, and going-away parties.

8. We can praise God not just with unadulterated joy but also when sorrow is a part of our emotional landscape.

9. Regardless of whether the participant was crying or shouting for joy, each person could praise God for fulfilling his promise to restore his people to their land; his faithfulness to them when they were in captivity; the freedom to worship him; their expectation that he would continue to provide for them in the future just as he had in the past; and restoring them despite their waywardness.

10. Praising God means acknowledging the Lord's attributes and admiring them. It also means recognizing the ways he has expressed those attributes in his relationship with you. As one ponders these things, one's heart rejoices, making the experience not just a mental exercise but also one that involves the emotions. As a result, laughter and tears, humility and happiness can be commingled. But most important, we are drawn closer to God and experience him in deeper ways.

Just for Fun. As the leader of the group, bring the local newspaper section that lists upcoming local events and festivities so the women can choose one during their time together. If your community is small, bring some papers from neighboring towns for the group to peruse as well.

LESSON TWO

Purpose: To discover ways to encounter God when alone so we can reflect him more appropriately when we reenter society.

2. The reminder that he knew Moses' name is a very intimate way for God to relate to Moses. It's like our learning and using another person's name, except in the Hebrew culture knowing a person's name was very personal. This information was not divulged lightly or quickly. The closeness that God insinuates with Moses is touching.

5. Moses apparently needed assurances that God would express his goodness to his people and to Moses, despite the people's behavior. The intimate

sharing of God's name followed by the statement that he shows mercy and compassion on those he chooses to reassures Moses of God's grace. Since these are the qualities he highlights rather than judgment, it suggests God will care for his people despite their waywardness.

6. God shows his love and respect for Moses by revealing his glory, much as we express our love by letting another see us in an intimate way. God also explains how he will protect Moses, which is an expression of love and respect. When someone does not feel love or respect, that person doesn't act in protective ways nor does he or she bother to explain actions. People in authority over us can sometimes be haughty or arrogant rather than loving and respectful. God, despite his authority over Moses, was neither haughty nor arrogant.

7. As we spend solitary time with God, we can express our hesitancies and concerns about life, explain what we think we need to fulfill his will and live honorably before him, and ask him to reveal himself to us. We can expect him to respond with an unveiling of some characteristics we hadn't seen so clearly before and to give us a deeper sense of his love and respect for us. In short, we will more richly experience God.

8. Moses came away with direction from God on how to lead a godly life. We can expect the same.

9. We can expect, when we encounter God in ways that transform our hearts and encourage our spirits, that we, too, will be radiant—though certainly not to the degree Moses was. But our faces will reflect God's glory.

10. We can look at Jesus' life to learn more about who God is, and we also have the Holy Spirit living inside us to reveal God's character to us. Moses didn't have Jesus or the Spirit to help him to understand and experience God.

   Praying Together. Have slips of paper to pass out to each woman.

LESSON THREE

Purpose: To learn how to give out of obedience and faith, discovering more about God in the process.

3. The disciples were probably tired, hungry, overwhelmed by the needs of such a large crowd, feeling inadequate to the task of giving to so many, eager to send the crowd away to have the people satisfy their own needs and leave the disciples alone to rest.

4. John 6:9 tells us the food belonged to a boy. He was probably hungry and looking forward to his lunch! But he was eager to know more about Jesus, and willing to contribute all he had in obedience to him.

5. Jesus wanted to teach the disciples to think beyond the obvious solutions (going into town and buying enough food to feed the crowd) and

to look to God to provide from what is readily available (the little food they already had). Despite the disciples' hard hearts, God blessed the little to create much. This story teaches us that (1) when we give in faith and obedience, God will multiply; (2) God is eager to satisfy us spiritually and physically; and (3) when we rely utterly on him, we will experience him in ways we never would otherwise.

7. Jesus wants us to bring generous, open hearts to our relationship with him.

8. God is generous-hearted and patient with us, willing to teach us a lesson through different experiences if the first one didn't "take." Obviously, the storm and the disciples' fear would make them more eager to learn. In a sense, God "squeezed their hearts" through fearful circumstances to create greater receptivity. We shouldn't be surprised when he does the same with us.

9. We can imagine that the child experienced the joy of being used by God in ways the boy could never have imagined: the blessing of his meager offering being multiplied when he chose to give it away; the growth of his faith; a deeper sense of who God is and what he is capable of; the reward of seeing others provided for and blessed through his giving; a lesson in what can happen when a person obeys God with a generous heart; a moment to remember for the rest of his life. In a sense, the boy's sacrifice was a gift that "has kept on giving." Even today we can learn from it.

   Friendship Boosters. Have a sheet of paper for each woman.

LESSON FOUR

Purpose: To explore how God blesses us and reveals himself to us when we wrestle with him.

4. Jacob showed tenacity, brashness, courage, pridefulness, boldness, a foolish lack of fear, and pigheadedness. He was determined to get from this heavenly being what he wanted—a blessing. He was prepared to hang on for as long as necessary.

5. Jacob's attempt to get someone to do what he wants fails this time. He received a blessing not because he demanded it, but because God wanted to give it. While it may appear that Jacob was winning the wrestling match, the ease with which the Lord touches Jacob's limb and wounds him shows that God could have bested Jacob at any point he chose. Jacob acknowledges that God spared his life. Perhaps for the first time Jacob realizes that God blesses his children who wrestle with him not because they wrestle well but because God wants to use the feisty encounter to transform the wrestler.

6. Jacob's limp served as a reminder to Jacob (and Jewish people to this day) that to encounter God is to be transformed. We are never the same

after being touched by him. Every day Jacob's limp reinforced that God chose to place his hand of blessing on Jacob. The physical touch signified a spiritual transformation and marked Jacob as chosen by God. Changing Jacob's name to "Israel" also served as a marker that God had a special plan for Jacob, the father of the Israelites.

Friendship Boosters. Bring a book of names that provides the meaning of each name to the group.

LESSON FIVE

Purpose: To realize that a humble response to God will bring us closer to him, while arrogance and disobedience form wedges between God and us.

2. Despite being snubbed by a group of troublemakers and skeptics, Saul rested in God's opinion of him. He could have had his enemies wiped out right there, which would have secured his position. Instead, he made no comment on the group of rabble-rousers and surrounded himself with "valiant men whose hearts God had touched." Saul exhibits an awareness of the importance of his companions having vital spiritual lives.

4. Samuel had made it clear to Saul that his primary responsibility as king wasn't defeating armies or governing the Israelites but simple obedience—he was to do whatever God directed. But Saul three separate times (in 1 Samuel 13:7–14; 15:17–23; and 28:1–19) felt compelled to make "adjustments" to God's commands. His actions showed pride in his own judgment, overzealousness to express his power, and a haughtiness that made him think he didn't need to obey *all* God commanded. Perhaps saddest of all was his seeming inability to understand why his actions were unacceptable to God; he had rationalized his behavior to such a degree that he could no longer understand what his divine mandate was.

5. While Saul admits his wrongdoing, he seems more concerned with appearances and maintaining his position than in his relationship with God. This seems especially true in verse 30 when he asks Samuel to make a public appearance with him.

7. A responsive heart to God is: obedient; humble; eager to please God; able to see one's own sin; willing to confess when wrongdoing is exposed; able to discern one's weaknesses and address them; open to criticism and capable of learning from it. A heart that pulls away from God is disobedient, sometimes in seemingly minor things; proud; indifferent to God; incapable of seeing sin or flaws; and angered by criticism.

Just for Fun. Bring slips of paper for each woman and a heart-red object to put the papers in.

LESSON SIX

Purpose: To experience God more fully by applying his grace to our lives and by extending it to others.

1. Encourage the participants to keep their stories to a few minutes each. If someone's story goes on too long, politely ask her to conclude it so others will have enough time to tell their stories.

4. Saul might very well have thought

   - I killed several of God's messengers.
   - I was completely wrong about Jesus; he really is God.
   - I have led so many other people astray with my zealousness.
   - How can I ever make amends?
   - How can I ever find forgiveness?
   - I deserve God's punishment of this blindness, for I have indeed been spiritually blind.
   - How will God tell me what to do now? What will he ask me to do?

5. God wants us to take the time to examine our hearts and to recognize how utterly dependent we are on his grace and mercy. If he does not extend these to us, we will remain lost.

6. God will put us in situations in which we are forced to face aspects of ourselves we would rather not acknowledge. But it is only after we see our lostness that God saves us.

7. God asks a hard thing of Ananias: to be gracious to an enemy who has been eager to kill Christ's followers; to believe God's grace could change a murderous heart; to trust God's grace to be sufficient for Ananias if Saul chose to have Ananias killed after he revealed himself to be a Christian.

8–9. If one thing was true of Jewish people in Scripture, it is that they were pleased to be God's chosen and not eager to share that appellation with others. Despite God's constant goading for them to spread the good news about God, the Jews were not interested in responding. By the time the church was beginning, even Jews who became Christians viewed Jesus as a Jewish Messiah. They found the idea of Jesus dying for Jews and Gentiles alike anathema. Hence Ananias must have been mystified—at the very least—by God's statement that Saul would spread the gospel to the Gentiles. Ultimately, God's entire message to Ananias makes no sense to the man: "Go to a mortal enemy and heal him because he will take the gospel to the Gentiles. Oh, yeah, and to the Jews as well." Ananias's response is fraught with faith and courage.

10. Saul had the opportunity to extend God's grace to others as he preached about Jesus. That message of grace was received by some, for verse 25 indicates that "his followers" helped him escape death. Saul also needed to extend grace to those who wished to kill him. Of course, only a few

days before, he, too, was killing Christians. The disciples, his new brothers in Christ, were also in need of grace from Saul. They were slow to believe God had transformed the murderous man into, of all things, an evangelist! These situations taught Saul how we all need grace—not just those who have to be struck blind by God to see the light, but also the people in the crowd, the zealous Jews, and those already following Christ. We all have gone astray in one way or another.

11. Some principles about grace are as follows:
   - It is not something we can earn, regardless of how zealous we are.
   - God wants us to see how needy we are so he can satisfy that need.
   - Not only do we need grace, but we also need to extend it to others. If we cannot do that, then we do not really understand grace.
   - We can only experience grace when we are humble (or have been humbled, as in Saul's case).
   - Grace is central in our relationship with God. Jesus communicated a very simple message to Saul: You've messed up; now I'll fix it. As we acknowledge the former and watch the latter, we are seeing grace in action. Of course, the "fixing up" doesn't mean our past actions are nullified. (The people Saul murdered weren't brought back to life.) Instead, we, the sinner, are fixed up—forgiveness and mercy are given. And we experience that grace each time we confess our sins. Each time we do, we love the Lord all the more for extending grace to us once again.

Friendship Boosters. Bring a variety of colored pieces of chalk or large sheets of paper, tape, and crayons, depending on the weather.

FAITH

Women of Faith Bible studies are based on the popular
Women of Faith conferences.

Women of Faith is partnering with Zondervan Publishing House,
Integrity Music, *Today's Christian Woman* magazine, and Campus Crusade
to offer conferences, publications, worship music, and inspirational gifts
that support and encourage today's Christian women.

Since their beginning in January of 1996, the Women of Faith conferences
have enjoyed an enthusiastic welcome by women across the country.

Call 1-888-49-FAITH for the many conference locations and dates available.

www.women-of-faith.com

**See the following page for additional information
about Women of Faith products.**

Look for these faith-building resources from Women of Faith:

Friends Through Thick & Thin by Gloria Gaither, Peggy Benson,
  Sue Buchanan, and Joy Mackenzie
    Hardcover 0-310-21726-1

We Brake for Joy! by Patsy Clairmont, Barbara Johnson, Marilyn Meberg,
  Luci Swindoll, Sheila Walsh, and Thelma Wells
    Hardcover 0-310-22042-4

Bring Back the Joy by Sheila Walsh
    Hardcover 0-310-22023-8
    Audio Pages 0-310-22222-2

The Joyful Journey by Patsy Clairmont, Barbara Johnson,
  Marilyn Meberg, and Luci Swindoll
    Softcover 0-310-22155-2
    Audio Pages 0-310-21454-8

Joy Breaks by Patsy Clairmont, Barbara Johnson,
  Marilyn Meberg, and Luci Swindoll
    Hardcover 0-310-21345-2

Women of Faith Journal
    Journal 0-310-97634-0

Promises of Joy for Women of Faith
    Gift Book 0-310-97389-9

Words of Wisdom for a Woman of Faith
    Gift Book 0-310-97390-2

Prayers for a Woman of Faith
    Gift Book 0-310-97336-8